Tenant Representation Network

BONUS CHAPTERS

1. What is Tenant Representation Network?

Tenant Representation Network ("TRN") is a network much like CCIM (Certified Commercial Investment Member) or SIOR (Society of Industrial and Office Realtors). TRN was established to bring heavy knowledge to those that want to specialize in a particular niche, product, and market to truly become the sharpest in their fields and viewed in the highest regard among peers and clients. The tenant representation segment of the commercial real estate industry has grown from an idea out of many top brokerage firms and professionals around the turn of the century, and has now exploded in recognition from Fortune 500 companies down to your local clients that serve your markets.   TRN is growing in recognition, members and, education. TRN will continue to evolve and provide promising insight for those that want the highest degree of knowledge. In the information age, knowledge is king. TRN will arm you to leverage this knowledge to better represent clients nationally and internationally.

2. Why become an exclusive tenant rep?

The information age combined with the internet provides consumers with greater transparency and access and commercial real estate is starting to feel the effects. It won't be long before some of the loose dual agency regulations become more stringent; it's already happening in certain states. This major factor dual agency does not create a winning side; someone has to win, and someone has to lose. By reading this book you are either reading for competitive advantage or you are reading to dominate as a tenant rep broker. As you become more versed as a tenant rep we encourage you to better understand the landlord listing broker's perspective from a principle standpoint, as well as, a literal standpoint.

By clearly defining that you are a tenant rep, your mind focuses on the client, friend, and individual. You become very aware that your job is to create the greatest outcome for your client so they will use you over and over.

Two amazing things go with focusing on tenant representation. First, very large scale organizations and fortune 500 companies have in-house real estate divisions but they outsource tenant reps. The reason is the power a tenant rep can bring to a specific product category and target market. By being the professional for their negotiation need, you will continue to win for them, thus winning more clients with past proven results, and benefit your career by being laser focused on tenant representation. Second, it's not being a listing broker! New office listings, old office listings, portfolio changes, listings brokers on rarely get a chance to feel the excitement of enjoying the wild ride a start up or mature company goes through in their business lifetimes.

3. What is an exclusive tenant rep and daily life?

An exclusive tenant rep is a real estate agent or broker who exclusively represents a user of space as an integral partner or consultant in the identification of their required location, space, and type of building. You will serve and advise your clients on many facets, such as, coordinating the layout design particular to the client's needs, negotiating on behalf of the tenant for terms, rental rate, concessions, options and a multitude of issues and factors for the tenant's benefit. Often times, you are assisting in referring office furniture, wiring, move coordination and other vendor related services. Throughout your client's tenancy you will be available to advise on many issues, including, expense pass-through's, issues with the landlord or management, expansions and contractions, lease buyouts, and lease renewals.

Below is an outline of an example day in the life of an Exclusive Tenant Representative. This is a very basic daily plan but gives you the sense of the strategy and routine one lives. Demographics and products type changes these in multiple ways.

6:30 a.m.: You should be already awake scanning for any emails that are important that can be handled with a simple email or with remembered deal points. Then enjoy reading up on your local economy, macro economy, new technologies, the stock market, as well as best practice emails from sites such as LinkedIn and National Association of Realtor type sites.

8:00 a.m.: Most are in the office checking voicemails, answering emails that are time critical and getting ready to sit down with their senior partners or partners to discuss what is most immediate, then preparing to pitch for new business. Talk with anyone that works close or in your immediate market and find out if they have any new offers or deals that they have heard of or rumors for prospects to go after. Talk with your admin and marketing team if there is anything outstanding that needs immediate attention to finish such as up to the minute presentation materials.

9:00 a.m.: Begin cold calling, cold marketing, and cold networking. Focus on creating and setting appointments with decision makers. Tenant Representation is a very lucrative niche so you have to assume any company of significant value has many competing tenant reps firms networking and pitching for their business. You need to know your competition too, where they work, what they focus on and what they have done to win business. 20% of the brokers in each market do 80% of the big deals so find out everything you can to eliminate the competition. As you head to 12:00 ask the immediate prospect if you can take that decision maker out to lunch that day. Lunch should be all business at least five days a week.

12:00 p.m.: Lunch time, time to meet with a prospective client, valuable co worker, meet with a complementary business owner to double approach a new client, make sure you fill the 200 working lunch days with advanced business initiatives.

1:00 p.m.: Review any emails, voicemails, documents on your desk from admin/marketing as you get ready to prospect and prospect. Also during this time make sure lease and purchase details are being completed with asset managers, escrow officers, accounting checks, insurance providers, architects etc. Typically hard prospecting is done in the morning where there are zero administration functions but mid afternoon prospecting is a hybrid of prospecting and tying up loose ends.

5:00 p.m.: Finishing the day strong really ends with meeting with your team or partner to recap on the day and what is in store the following day. Also if there is any industry event or time to meet one last potential client or complementary entity this is the time to meet while the rest of the world sits in Traffic.

4. Pitching for reasons to use Tenant Representation

Any company that considers themselves of value will use a Tenant Rep Broker but some companies slip through the cracks and do not know the full benefits of a Tenant Rep Broker. Business owners know their industry inside and out which is why you benefit knowing commercial real estate inside and out. Business owners know payroll is traditionally the highest cost per month then rental costs and tenant reps know rental costs COLD. Business owners might only negotiate a lease every 3 to 5 years, where you do hourly. Typical landlords negotiate and work on leases daily or weekly or monthly so a company negotiating a lease every 3 to 5 years is absolutely in the dark on current month pricing and deal points. Tenant Reps can find out if the landlord is pretending they do not need a company when in fact they are desperate. For example in a multi tenant office building, if the owner has 20 tenants with 8 tenants lease expiring in the same year the owner is more inclined to work the best deals for the first ones to renew, blend and extend or lease amend.

Another value a tenant rep brings to the table is reviewing space plans, double blind IT bids, knowledge of competition and complementary businesses in certain areas, tax incentive zones, zoning issues, city planning issues, an most important being the middle man to reduce any tense issues Landlord and Tenants go through constantly......for FREE!

Once landlord's finds out a company gets smart and writes the landlord or owners representative they are no longer speaking directly, noting they are using a tenant rep broker, a company will now begin to save on time of negotiating which that time would be better spent on growing the business. Next the tenant rep broker comes in like a surgeon and flattens the negotiation with rental comps, relocation opportunities, ownership intelligence, and other side cost savings such as lease review and comments.

The court system in almost all parts or the world can have representatives for both sides, so does commercial real estate.

5. How to Qualify the Tenant

When prospecting for new business sometimes you hook a fish that is not a fish but weeds. You need to qualify every prospect and current clients to make sure you are using the best use of the only thing you own...TIME. Use N.U.M.E.R.A.L for one of your qualifiers and you will grow in efficiency and income.

NEED – What is the Clients need? If Office and you focus on office...GREAT!

URGENCY – What is the time frame of that need?

MOTIVATION – Why the need for this commercial real estate action?

EXPECTATION – What are their expectations of the market today and near future?

RESOURCES – Do they have the capacity or proof of funds to make this action work?

AUTHORITY – Is this the decision maker that has done deals before or approved to decide and sign?

LOYALTY – Has the client seen locations already or signed a Representation Agreement?

6. How a Tenant qualifies you.

Below is what most tenants look for when meeting you for the first time and interacting with you before they agree to working with you.

1) They need to know you understand their product type being it industrial, retail, biotech, etc. You need to know it cold.
2) Quick and Quality communication, CEO's are used to everyone responding as quickly as possible and as a non employed real estate arm to the CEO or decision maker you need to be on your toes with quick and quality phone or email correspondences.
3) You need to know the market they want to be in the future cold, and if you do not know that market, pull someone in that does immediately.
4) Provide amazing examples of your past experiences for any reason to benefit you and if you have to bring in someone more experienced do so.

7. Know your market Cold

Know your market inside and out. How many businesses, how many buildings, how many zoning codes, how many competing agents, the average square foot size of the tenants, etc. Being the go to guy for your market will enable you to stack up more business as well as receive in bound referrals from agents, brokers, banks, clients that know you are the dominator for this market. Join associations in your market, meet community board members, and get involved in that community. A lot of CEO's that drive to this market live within miles of their market and they too go to community events, meetings, professional meetings to further their businesses.

8. Focus on a product type (s)

Being known for a specific product type such as office can also exponentially force your mind and your clients to think about you and your market dominance niche. Make it a point to note the markets you work and the product type you specialize in, this will subliminally force you to evolve and strengthen your niche success. Your specialization will also grow in understanding your client's economic cycles, business partners, economic trends, typically net and gross margins, and how you can be another pair of eyes for them for possible acquisition or growth opportunities. Now you become an even more specialized value proposition to be remembered when the need arises.

9. Lease Comparables

One way to earn new business is to update your existing and prospective clients about what is going on in the market in regards to what the last 5-10 lease deals were within a certain zip code or territory. Businesses will remember that you have relevant up to date information and will remember you and will enjoy reading your emails.

10.   Lease Expiration Dates

Lease expiration dates are critical to a business, the faster you find out when a company's lease expires the faster you will be able to help them. Time is critical in real estate, over 90% of businesses finish out a lease term, some may renew early or "blend and extend" but if you can contact a tenant 6-12 months before their expiration your chances of winning their business rises dramatically. Some of the best ways to find lease expiration dates is to contact the company and ask..."When Does your Lease Expire". Secondly if you work for a major firm you should have a research department with thousands of lease expirations they pull from leases and articles from newspapers. Owners appreciate you knowing their lease expiration time frames, and annual increases so they are not caught off guard, and what you can do today to benefit their rental budgets.

11.   Letters Of Intent

The letter of intent is for a mutual understanding where the misunderstood email and verbal offerings of the past are eliminated. Letter of intents are much more professorial, precise and leave less room for lease comments to kill a deal. Letter of intents are almost all nonbinding, a moot point between two parties agreeing to a set amount of terms and conditions that both parties would enjoy over a set period of time.

Also, the letter of intent world is always changing, for example, in the early 2000's we had language regarding dedicated single pass air closets for server racks. Millions of tenants in the 21st Century were in absolute need of a server rack closet for a number of competitive advantages but in the "teens" of the 21st Century we use much more affordable services with companies such as Amazon Cloud that continue to eliminate the need for server closet language in letter of intent forms.

Today a Letter Of Intent would look like this below. Letter of Intents vary from State to State, city to city but this should give you a solid review of Letter of Intents.

1) RE: "Regarding" Shows the meaning of the entire Letter Of Intent

RE: PROPOSAL TO LEASE / XXXXX XXXXX & ASSOCIATES Inc.

2) The offering that describes both parties entities that would be reflected on the lease.

Dear Michael: On behalf of XXXXX XXXXX & ASSOCIATES Inc. ("Tenant"), we are pleased to present the following non-binding proposal, outlining terms upon which XXXX XXXX LP ("Landlord") may proceed to enter into a binding Lease agreement.

3) Use of the company's operations will have to be clearly defined so the ownership knows full well what is going to be run out of this suite. Begin with being general who provides an advantage to your client seeing you are trying for the maximum amount of uses in case the business decides to reinvent themselves as most companies do in their desired business niche.

USE: The Premises shall be used in connection with Tenant's psychiatric practice, as permitted by City of San Diego.

4) Describe the suite in question and its approximate size.

LOCATION AND SIZE PREMISES: Tenant shall lease Suite 130 consisting of approximately 6,384 rentable square feet. Most of your offerings will be suites of multi tenant properties so suite numbers are very crucial when an owner has multiple offers being negotiated on their building.

5) Length of lease term written in months or years.

LEASE TERM AND COMMENCEMENT OF RENT: The Lease Term shall be for sixty-three (63) months and the Commencement of Rent shall occur upon substantial completion of Tenant Improvements estimated to occur on or around January 1, 2017.

6) BASE RENT: Here you write out the rental rate and utilities as well as follow with numerical numbering for clarity. Next you describe the annual increases so your tenant is fully aware of the CPI (consumer price index) increases which most small to medium sized businesses dislike to see but your goal is to educate the client that 90% of the properties in your market area have CPI or fixed annual increases.

BASE RENT: The Base Rent shall be three dollars and fifty cents ($3.50) per rentable square foot per month, Full Service Gross, net of electricity. The Base Rent, net of electricity, shall include janitorial, insurance, taxes and standard heating/air conditioning during building standard hours. The Base Rent shall increase annually on the anniversary of the commencement date by a fixed three percent (3%).

7) Early Occupancy or Early Access is typically a grace period of 30 days but is always negotiable.

EARLY ACCESS: Provided that a Lease has been mutually executed and that Tenant does not interfere with Landlord's contractor in the timely completion of Tenant Improvements, Tenant shall have the right to access any portion of the Premises up to thirty days (30) days prior to the Lease Commencement for the purposes of installing furniture, fixtures and equipment. Tenant shall not be required to pay Base Rent or utility costs for the Premises during this Early Access period.

8) Free Rent with a qualified credit tenant should be equal to one free month a year which can be negotiated inside or outside of the lease.

RENTAL ABATEMENT: Tenant shall not be required to pay Base Rent during months two (2) through six (6) of the initial Lease Term.

9) Renewal options predominantly favors the tenants side of the negotiation so an owner will most likely want to keep the renewal times short, much higher renewal rental rate over base year, and or the landlord will work to eliminate from the negotiations. Depending on the type of client, product type, and if the tenant is the type to sell the business, owners must be careful not to give too much on renewals.

Option To Renew: Upon expiration of the lease, provided Tenant is and has not been in default of the lease, Tenant shall have one (1) option to renew the lease for an additional five (5) years at the then current fair market rent with no less than six (6) and no more than nine (9) months prior written notice to Landlord.

10) Tenant improvements can be one of the largest and most time consuming and critical events in a landlord and tenant negotiation. Make sure every detail is in the initial offering so there are no surprises that could ruin progressive negotiations.

TENANT IMPROVEMENTS: Utilizing building standard materials and subject to a mutually acceptable space plan, Landlord shall provide "turnkey" Tenant Improvement's for the Premises, not to exceed $45.00 per usable square foot. Said improvements shall include:

Turnkey

- Seven perimeter private offices;

- A conference room (excluding floor core);

- Kitchenette with VCT Tile, sink, refrigerator, dishwasher and 5' of upper and lower cabinets;

- New Carpet and New Paint Throughout to match company colors

Landlord's Tenant Improvement Allowance shall NOT be used towards any costs associated with space planning, construction drawings, permits, general contractor's fee and construction management fee.

11) Check with your states assignment and subleasing laws. Some states do not even require a tenant to negotiate assignments or subleases because a tenant obtains these by right.

ASSIGNMENT AND SUBLEASING: Per the standard Lease agreement.

12) Signage can sometimes be key to a company's image and success. Make sure you describe the goal of signage, where located, and how large. Most landlords will have little say in signage seeing it's dictated by the city signage standards laws.

SIGNAGE: Landlord shall provide building top signage, monument signage, and suite identification signage and add Tenant's name to the building directory, at Tenant's sole cost and expense.

13) Operating Expenses are negotiable, sometimes even thrown out for the ideal tenant. If Operating Expenses are not taken out or negotiated they typically look standard or boilerplate as below.

OPERATING EXPENSES: Tenant will be responsible for it's pro rata share of any operating expense increase in excess of the actual expenses incurred by Landlord during the calendar year ending December 31, 2XXX. Operating expenses shall include, but are not limited to, Landlord's cost of maintaining the Building, common and parking areas of the project, taxes, janitorial, insurance, utilities, building standard HVAC service, etc. In the event the building is not fully occupied at time of adjustment, operating expenses may be adjusted as if the Building was ninety five percent (95%) occupied for all years, including the base year.

14) HEATING VENTILATING AND AIR CONDITIONING: Make sure you confirm with the tenant the typical hours of operation before submitting the Letter of Intent. For tenants in an "around the clock" call center or emergency center it is crucial to have operators 24 hours a day. Make sure to bring the advantage of the landlord being responsible for HVAC issues.

HEATING VENTILATING AND AIR CONDITIONING AND OPERATING HOURS: Standard heating, ventilating and air conditioning shall be provided from 6:30 AM to 6:30 PM Monday through Friday, holidays excluded, and 8:00 AM to 1:00 PM on Saturday. After hours heating, ventilating and air conditioning will be provided upon request at Landlord's standard hourly charge. Any HVAC charges outside of normal business hours will be charged at market rate of $45 an hour.

15) FIRT MONTH'S RENT/SECURITY DEPOSIT : Typically Rent and Security mirrors leasing a residential property, meaning first and last month's rent. However when a tenant has shaky credit or it's a start up, the landlord will most likely require two or three months of security deposit. If a larger deposit is requested work to have the extra months of security deposit returned as the tenant pays on time for a certain amount of months.

FIRT MONTH'S RENT/SECURITY DEPOSIT: Upon execution of the Lease, Tenant shall pay to Landlord the first month's Base Rent and a Security Deposit subject to the Landlord's review of Tenant's financial statements.

16) Parking in major cities is very tight; a tough negotiator should be able to get better than standard parking costs for their client or a couple free reserved spaces. Parking is sometimes an oversight on a tenant's list of major items needed. It is important to make sure parking is covered before touring for ideal locations.

PARKING: Available on a first-come, first-serve basis, Tenant shall be required to lease four (4) unreserved parking spaces per one thousand (1,000) usable square feet of the Premises leased. All unreserved parking stalls shall be at the prevailing Building rate which is currently $40 per stall, per month. All surface visitor parking stalls are currently free of charge and available on a first-come, first-serve basis. All surface visitor parking stalls may be subject to parking charges in the future.

17) DO NOT FORGET ADDING THIS BROKERAGE COMMISSION LANGUAGE, some brokers' keep this language separate which is sometimes ideal. To keep separate, type a letter of intent on behalf of your brokerage directly for the owner/listing broker to sign thus eliminating brokerage fees in the letter of intent.

BROKERS: XXXX, Inc. represents the Landlord and XXXXXX XXXXXXXX represents the Tenant in this transaction. Upon execution of the Lease by Landlord and Tenant, XXXXXX XXXXXXXX shall be paid a leasing fee equal to four percent (4%) of the total Base Rent consideration for months one (1) through sixty-three (63) of the Lease Term. Payment of said leasing fee shall be one-half (1/2) upon execution of a lease by Landlord and Tenant, and one-half (1/2) upon the commencement date.

18) Keeping strong contingencies that are a disadvantage to the owner can help keep the strength of the negotiations in your corner as the landlord agrees to challenging contingencies that can increase tenant negotiations on multiple levels. Time and making sure you are the only one to negotiate on the space can increase a tenant's outcome.

CONTINGENCIES: This proposal, unless accepted in writing, shall become null and void at 5:00 p.m. on Friday, October 10, 2XXX, and shall be specifically contingent upon: The availability of the subject space. It is understood that the Premises may not be shown to other prospects and Landlord will not pursue all other offers to lease Premises.

19) Keep all events confidential. The first competing Tenant Rep broker to see your secret negotiating sauce or what the final outcome was on your lease or purchase situation can leave a less favorable scenario. Make sure you provide zero insight to the street about your deals unless you scored the deal of a lifetime. Being shown up by another competitor for something you have no control over is one

more avenue of losing credit. For example some owners give amazing deals to companies they take stock in thus making some deals look 50% better than your outcome.

CONFIDENTIAL: Tenant acknowledges that the terms and conditions contained herein and details of the ensuing negotiations will remain confidential between the parties to the lease and no proposals, lease drafts, leases or summaries of any kind will be distributed, copied or otherwise transmitted, orally or in writing, to any other entity or person.

ALL INFORMATION INCLUDED IN THIS PROPOSAL PERTAINING TO XXXXXX—INCLUDING BUT NOT LIMITED TO ITS OPERATIONS, EMPLOYEES, TECHNOLOGY AND CLIENTS—ARE PROPRIETARY AND CONFIDENTIAL, AND ARE SUPPLIED WITH THE UNDERSTANDING THAT THEY WILL BE HELD IN CONFIDENCE AND NOT DISCLOSED TO THIRD PARTIES WITHOUT THE PRIOR WRITTEN CONSENT OF XXXXXX. THIS LETTER/PROPOSAL IS INTENDED SOLELY AS A PRELIMINARY EXPRESSION OF GENERAL INTENTIONS AND IS TO BE USED FOR DISCUSSION PURPOSES ONLY. THE PARTIES INTEND THAT NEITHER SHALL HAVE ANY CONTRACTUAL OBLIGATIONS TO THE OTHER WITH RESPECT TO THE MATTERS REFERRED HEREIN UNLESS AND UNTIL A DEFINITIVE AGREEMENT HAS BEEN FULLY EXECUTED AND DELIVERED BY THE PARTIES. THE PARTIES AGREE THAT THIS LETTER/PROPOSAL IS NOT INTENDED TO CREATE ANY AGREEMENT OR OBLIGATION BY EITHER PARTY TO NEGOTIATE A DEFINITIVE LEASE/PURCHASE AND SALE AGREEMENT AND IMPOSES NO DUTY WHATSOEVER ON EITHER PARTY TO CONTINUE NEGOTIATIONS, INCLUDING WITHOUT LIMITATION ANY OBLIGATION TO NEGOTIATE IN GOOD FAITH OR IN ANY WAY OTHER THAN AT ARM'S LENGTH. PRIOR TO DELIVERY OF A DEFINITIVE EXECUTED AGREEMENT, AND WITHOUT ANY LIABILITY TO THE OTHER PARTY, EITHER PARTY MAY (1) PROPOSE DIFFERENT TERMS FROM THOSE SUMMARIZED HEREIN, (2) ENTER INTO NEGOTIATIONS WITH OTHER PARTIES AND/OR (3) UNILATERALLY TERMINATE ALL NEGOTIATIONS WITH THE OTHER PARTY HERETO.

12.   Understanding Each Type of Commercial Lease

As a tenant, it is important to understand the type of lease structure the landlord is proposing and how it will impact your bottom line. There are 3 primary types of leases – Gross, Full Service and Net – as well as modified versions of each.

Gross Lease: A lease in which the tenant pays a flat sum for rent out of which the landlord must pay all expenses such as taxes, insurance, maintenance, utilities, etc.. Under this lease structure, the tenant is responsible for paying the stated rental rate only; all other expenses are borne by the landlord.

Full Service Lease: A lease which the tenant pays an all-inclusive rental rate which includes operating expenses and real estate taxes for the first year or the "Base Year". Under this lease structure, the tenant pays the base rent in the first year, and is also responsible for reimbursing the landlord for any costs over a Base Year or a predetermined Expense Stop.

Variations of the Gross or Full Service lease

Sub-variants of Gross (i.e. a "Modified Gross" lease) or Full Service Leases will feature much of the same structure outlined above, but have one or more expense items which are excluded from the clause. For instance, an industrial Modified Gross lease could require that the tenant pay for utilities and/or real estate taxes in addition to their Base Rent.

Net Lease Indicates a lease in which the stated rent excludes the insurance, utilities, operating expenses and real estate taxes for the building. The tenant is then responsible for the payment of some (or all) of these costs either directly or as Additional Rent. Under this lease structure, the tenant is responsible for paying their Base Rent, as well as certain operating expenses and real estate taxes.

Variations of the Net lease

Sub-variants of the Net Lease structure include Modified Net, Double Net or Triple Net.

Modified Net and Double Net are instances where most operating expenses are paid directly by or reimbursed by (an expense "Pass Throughs") the Tenant. For example, the tenant could be responsible for their own utilities and reimbursing the landlord for Common Area Maintenance ("CAM"), but the landlord is solely responsible for paying the real estate tax bill.

Under a Triple Net or "NNN" Lease, the tenant is responsible for paying and/or reimbursing the landlord for all operating expenses and real estate taxes. Capital expenditures (i.e. expenses which are typically depreciated over a period of greater than 12 months) are usually excluded from the property's operating costs, but it depends on exactly how the lease defines capital expenditures.

A fourth, less common lease structure is a Percentage Rent structure whereby the rental payment is based upon a percentage of the tenant's sales volume. This lease structure is usually used in retail environments. Percentage rent can be used in tandem with a lease structure above, whereby the tenant pays Base Rent and a percentage of sales.

Understanding exactly what your lease's structure is an important variable in determining the most cost effective lease proposal.

13.   Conditional Use Permit

If you get into a situation where a Conditional Use Permit or "CUP" is needed make sure you get a head start before touring the client through any property. Conditional Use permits are very specific and it's immediately encouraged to call your local city planning department and speak directly with the cities CUP division.

The purpose of a Conditional Use Permit is for tenants not allowed in certain areas by right but with certain rights that come with restrictions. These CUP Divisions are setup to establish a review process for the development of uses that may be desirable under appropriate circumstances, but are not permitted by right in the applicable zone. The intent of these procedures is to review these uses on a case by case basis to determine whether and under what conditions the use may be approved at a given location. This is to protect the safety and health of those surrounding the property in question.

The process for a Conditional Use Permit is to contact a CUP division planner about the type of tenant use and location and zoning and to review all required documents prior to any submittal. Next is to have the tenant submit the Conditional Use Permit application, complete and if needed provide supporting documentation. If everything is correct and the CUP division is accepting it moves to a public hearing at which the City Hearing Officer will review and provide insight to allow or deny the request.

Next the CUP division planner will send out by mail public notices within a 300-1000 foot radius at the cost of the tenant for anyone to protest which they will have roughly 10 days. If no protests or issues the decision by the City Hearing Officer can approve or deny at the final city board meeting. The entire process may take roughly ten to twelve weeks and cost an average of ten thousand dollars per application fee which could be seen as a short, low-cost win to tenants that need to be in a certain area for success.

14.   Finding and Building Business

One the biggest ways to building business in commercial real estate is to learn the business and experience the business as fast as possible. Meaning you need to jump right in, you cannot be part time in the beginning. Much like Wall Street, working for a large corporate firm to understand every single detail at a high paced level will help dramatically at achieving the powerful skills that will follow you for a lifetime. With that advice, Google top ten commercial tenant representation firms and start to interview to work underneath an experienced high producing tenant rep broker that has the need for a junior or associate agent.

Looking back at the answers we received from top producing tenant reps, cold knocking, cold calling, cold emailing, marketing, and social media were the top most beneficial ways to getting your name out and it is encouraged right from the day you start your career.

Tenant Representation is evolving constantly but the basics have always been the foundation. One Basic is the reminder to tenants that if you do not create the most favorable outcome the tenant should never use you again, meaning you must do the best for your clients every time. To make sure this is materializes, call, send emails and market your success (when allowed to use a client's deal) on how you consistently beat the market, enjoy growing networkable relationships that benefit the client.

If you work for a major firm, ask the research department to send you all the expirations on leases in the specific zip code or submarket that you want to focus in. For example: Office, Denver, 3,000-999,999 SF with expirations in the next 36 months. Then you can work to contact the owner through their website, online yellow pages, LinkedIn, Facebook, twitter, etc until you get a hold of the owner or find out who the decision maker is. Typically you will want to work a geographic area of 500 buildings with roughly 5000 businesses and work to represent the best and biggest of those 5000 businesses. Some just focus on national institutional tenants throughout the country and some focus on local credit companies that have significant commercial real estate space.

Over time you will begin to seek out what your ideal product, specialty, geography niche is and exploit that. For example most of the top performers consistently out perform other tenant reps when they focus on getting the business from one or two Fortune 500 clients and refer out the business to other tenants reps in other markets of the country or internationally. Other top performers work just representing Law Firms in a specific downtown market.

15.   Strategies for Strong Negotiations

Strategies for strong negotiations have changed, been eliminated and or added over time. Most tenant reps have seen all the tactics and strategies, some never, and some have forgotten. Here are some of the more classic strategies to create a better negotiating outcome.

1. Motivation – Find out why the subject property is available for lease, sublease, and sale. Find out what type the owner is, either a large portfolio holder, high net worth individual with deep pockets, an owner with other tenants leaving that could sweeten the outcome, or the owner is in a possible loan situation where the owner needs as much tenancy and income coming in to get their best loan.

2. Market Intelligence –Find out what the last three deals looked like in the building, then what the surrounding asking rate comparables looked like and what owners were provided on similar properties in the market. Comps can be found with listing platforms and third party vendors as well as searching online.

3. Use Leverage – One of the most beneficial ways to create leverage is to create a scenario that you have multiple better options without telling the owners representative but making sure they find out. If the owner's listing broker or representative works for a large commercial firm, talking to a colleague in that office about a couple offers you have with one particular client quickly gets back to the owner's representative in question. Also if an owner is a large portfolio holder and you have the opportunity to put offers on more than one of their properties it will insinuate that you are working on multiple properties.

16.   Market Intelligence

As we know tenant representation to be a lucrative avenue of real estate we cannot forget that there is always strong competition proposing, fighting, and negotiating for the business. One of the biggest ways to crush the competition is through market intelligence as mentioned before. Know exactly what deals are being done inside a specific building, specific area right down to if the owner is paying for the lighting and water. Some of the fastest ways to beat the competition is to find the best deals in the market today on the multiple listing services and present them ASAP. Contact every listing broker that works that specific market to what they have today and what is coming available in the next 60-90-120-150 days and what their owners are desperate to lease out as well as find out what owners are begging to construct as a build to suit option for prospective tenants. So many tenant reps forget large land owners can build a built to suit in time for a client that has a lease with a year or two left on their lease which is where you need to be in their lease expiration cycle.

The top talent knows price per square foot, owner incentives, above or below utility costs, strategy development, demographics, and employee savings through logistics and commute times, occupancy analysis and most of all leverage. Market Intelligence will give you extremely strong leverage and owners over time that see your name on their leases will know this and realize you are not going anywhere but up and will offer the best deals seeing they know you have more than one offer out on buildings that they may or may not own.

Also get to know project managers, developers, contractors, facility managers and banking facilitators that know which owners cannot be swayed and which can be leveraged. Everyone that touches a lease or negotiation in your market has some kind of market intelligence for you to help the client.

17.   Setting up the Tour

For some, touring is fun and easier than prospecting, but to some prospecting is easier and enticing than touring. Touring has a lot going on when dealing with a firm that has multiple C level decision makers that have to make time for a certain day. After questioning multiple top level tenant rep brokers, touring more than 6 properties the client will start to forget what they liked. We eat, breath, live real estate but almost all tenants do not. We can tour 20 locations and not feel what most call cloudiness, so make the top 6 the best on the list to tour or you will be out touring again which is very time consuming and will take away from other priorities.

Use services such as Google Maps that you can insert the multiple addresses and arrange them so you tour by time efficiency. Review Google Traffic to review the best times to tour which is typically after 1:00 p.m. when most people finish lunch and are back at work. Touring in the morning is not ideal, you fight rush hour, and morning is your ideal time for prospecting.

When talking to the listing brokers before the tour, make sure they are there and have the most updated flyers for you and your clients. They are the listing brokers, and are the most intimate with the building and most intimate with the owner. If a client wants immediate answers as most people today expect, they want instant answers. Therefore, having the listing broker to answer questions in person is a very strong way to see the motivation of the owners through the listing brokers mannerisms and answers.

18.   Percentage Rent Defined

Percentage rent in commercial real estate mostly equates to retail leasing. It is a fairly straight forward concept to national retail firms and franchised firms but to the new or mom and pop retail tenants, it could spell disaster if you are unfamiliar with retail real estate. Percentage rent is the devil in the detail scenario. There are natural break points, stipulated break point, inclusions and exclusions, overages, mandatory date deadlines so be prepared with reading the details.

Percentage Rent is very common in multi tenant retail parks with very visible retail pads. Owners enjoy having complementary companies come into a retail park so businesses can enjoy having the same shopper go door to door shopping. This is a premium to a tenant which the landlord is very well aware of. Sophisticated owners also rely on their listing brokers to know what the market rate for percentage rent is and what businesses typically generate in income so be very well versed in the tenants ordinary gross revenue, income, and expenses.

With natural break points, the owner would negotiate that roughly 5% of all sales will be paid monthly, or quarterly, or yearly. For example UPS that does $200,000 a month pays the owner $10,000 a month in gross sales a month. With a stipulated break point the owner requests if UPS does over $200,000 a month they get 5%, meaning UPS does $250,000 one month the owner receives $12,500 that month but if UPS does $200,000 or $180,000 or $150,000 the owner receives nothing. Work to get the owner to agree to the highest stipulated point possible, meaning UPS does $400,000 a month the owner gets 5% which almost all UPS stores will never reach.

19.   Common Area Factor: Rentable vs Usable Square Feet

Few commercial real estate concepts are as misunderstood by tenants and even real estate professionals, as the measurement of office space square footage for rent purposes. The formula to determine the amount of rent in most office leases incorporates both the usable square footage, plus the tenant's proportionate share of common areas in the building.

Usable Square Feet

In general, usable square footage is the amount of space you actually occupy. For smaller tenants, usable square footage is simply the area of the demised space inside your office suite with no exclusions for recess entry/exit doors or structural columns. What that means in essence, is that the space is measured as if columns are not there. But restrooms and janitor closets, elevator lobbies and public corridors are there, and you pay a portion of the space they occupy with the other tenants who use them.

For full floor or multi-floor tenants, usable square footage is everything inside the glass line, including restrooms, janitor closets or mechanical and electrical rooms. Like small tenants, full-floor or multi-floor tenants also must pay a share of the building common areas not on their floor, such as the main building lobby.

The Common Area Factor

The common area factor is a number which refers to shared spaces on a single floor, and within a building in its entirety. These spaces as previously mentioned can be a pro-rata share of tenant common areas such as restrooms and elevator lobbies, or main building lobbies and amenities which all tenants of the building use.

The Floor Common Area Factor refers to tenant common areas on that floor only, and although the number varies from building to building, it is generally near eight percent of the floor for a factor of 1.08.

The Building Common Area Factor refers to common areas for all the tenants in the building, and can range from six to eight percent. Common area factors determine the actual square footage for which a tenant will pay rent.

Typically when you are quoted a common area factor by the landlord or the building's leasing agent it includes the sum of the floor common area factor and the buildings common are factor. As a result for most office buildings the total common area factor ranges from 12 to 20% subject to the design of the building.

Rentable Square Feet

Simply stated, rentable square footage is the area of the enclosed interior space of the building other than holes in the floor, such as stairwells, and elevator and mechanical duct space. If you can stand on, you pay for it, because it is rentable space. That includes restrooms, janitor closets, electrical and telephone rooms, etc. What you pay for then–your rent–is the rentable square footage times the lease rate per square foot.

To calculate rentable square footage for a smaller (less than full-floor) tenant, first multiply the usable square footage by the floor common factor, then multiply that result by the building common factor.

Similarly, a full- or multi-floor tenant would multiply its full-floor usable by the building common factor because of the extra shared amenities and lobby space.

The Calculation

The formulas to determine the usf and the rsf are: rsf = usf x (1 + Add-on %)

Add-On % = (rentable sf / usable sf – 1)

For example: Assume you need 10,000 usf and there is a 15% add-on factor.

Rsf = 10,000 x (1 + .15) = 11,500 rsf

For example: Assume you a leasing 16,000 rsf and have 14,000 usf.

Add-On % = (16,000 / 14,000) – 1 = 14.29%

In some real estate markets a load or common area factor (CAF) is used instead of using an Add-On or Loss factor. Sometimes various landlords have differing definitions of these terms. It is a good practice to always clarify the calculation with the landlord or his agent to ensure there are no misunderstandings.

It is very important for a tenant to address this issue before a lease is signed, as there is usually little or no recourse after lease execution. Most leases do not detail a method of direct calculations of either usable or rentable square footage, and if a rentable figure is provided, it is almost always modified with the word "approximate." However, most reasonable landlords will accept a revision to lease language that the measurement of the premises will be verified by either the tenant's or landlord's architect subject to an acceptable measurement standard such as the BOMA Standard or the commonly accepted standard for the market. Your tenant representative should verify that the common area factor represented by the landlord is as fair and accurate as possible.

Comparing Various Buildings

When you are out evaluating space options it is important to note that most buildings have different common area factors and floor plate dimensions as shape can impact the space plan and the required amount of usable square footage. When comparing buildings particularly from a financial aspect you should be using a cost per usable square foot (USF) metric, to be sure you are evaluating your options on an "apples to apples" basis. Ultimately you are looking for the right space that not only fits your budget but also other real estate and workplace criteria. However, two buildings with the exact same face rental rate can have significantly different economics as a result of common area factors and space design efficiencies. Working with a tenant representation specialist who understands all the intricacies of leasing office space and possess the technical skills to evaluate various options will insure you are making an informed decision.

20.   Tenant Improvement Allowance

Get as much as you can, and maintain control of the build-out process. A key component of any lease negotiation is the tenant improvement allowance provided by the landlord to build-out or retrofit an office space for the tenant's specific use. The amount of the tenant improvement allowance, as well as the length of the lease term has a significant impact on the negotiated rental rate.

In addition to negotiating a favorable amount for tenant improvements provided by the Landlord, the ability to maintain control of the process is also important. Tenant Improvement allowances provided by the building owner to build-out or retrofit office space are typically structured in one of two ways:

1.   Turn Key Build-out: in this structure the Landlord covers all of the cost of the tenant build-out as part of the agreed upon rent and space plan generally outlining the scope of construction.

2.   Stated Dollar Amount: in this structure the Landlord provides a stated dollar amount for the tenant to use toward building out the space, often to include architectural and engineering fees.

When negotiating a lease, tenants would prefer not to come out of pocket for expenses related to building out the space. Many tenant rep brokers will often state their client wants a "turn-key" build out, but what they technically should strive for is to eliminate or minimize "out of pocket" costs for the tenant, as well as maximize the value of the improvement allowance, based on the rental rate that is negotiated.

The Problem with the Turn-Key Approach

The inherent issue with the turn-key build-out approach is that the Landlord is going to incorporate a significant amount of contingency cost into the construction cost estimates to prevent actual costs from exceeding the estimate. This could be a contingency as much as 25-30 percent, in effect creating the potential for another profit center for the Landlord, if they efficiently manage the build-out costs. In some cases "efficiently manage" could be construed as "cut corners".

For example, if the Landlord estimates the cost of the build-out at $35.00 per square foot, and that is the allowance, the negotiated rental rate is based upon, and ultimately the Landlord is able to build-out the space for $29.00 per square foot, then the tenant has given up $6.00 per square foot that could have gone towards improvements to their premises.

Another issue with the turn-key approach is that the tenant is relinquishing control of the tenant improvement dollars being spent on their space. Unless the tenant negotiates an extensively detailed work letter based on a detailed set of full construction plans, it is not uncommon to have surprises in the build-out that do not favor the tenant.

Maintaining Control of the Construction Process

In most cases it's preferred to negotiate a stated dollar amount for the tenant improvement allowance and maintaining as much control as possible over the build-out process. In addition, I request that the Landlord either waive or reduce their construction management fee, and allow the tenant to retain their own project manager to oversee the design and construction process. The objective is to shift control of the build-out from the Landlord to the Tenant which provides the ability to maintain quality control of the process and to insure the construction is completed on time to prevent any holdover rent fees in the case of relocation. Plus to have the control to "value engineer" as well as let the tenant reap the benefit of competitively bidding the construction contract to insure you get the most value out of your tenant improvement allowance.

If possible, it is also prudent to negotiate the right to amortize additional tenant improvement dollars into the rent should you decide to add additional improvements, upgrades or incur unexpected cost over-runs before you space is completed. You may elect to just to pay any costs over the allowance yourself, but it's nice to have that option. In cases, where the scope of work only involves new carpet, paint and moving a wall or two, having more control of the process is not as critical. However, in any significant interior construction job, it is highly recommended that you retain your own project manager, who will typically capture savings that benefit the tenant rather than the landlord that far exceed the fee charged by the project manager.

Choosing the stated improvement allowance approach requires more up-front work to insure the proper allowance is negotiated, but maintaining control of the construction process allows the tenant to realize the benefits of potential cost savings and maximize the value of their improvement allowance.

21.   Client Financial Analysis

Financial health is very important to creating a strong negotiated outcome. Financial analysis helps in understanding the past, current and future projections of your client. Your goal is to be more than a trusted commercial advisor but a skilled financial advisor when it comes to financial statements to pitch to the listing brokers and ownership how rock solid your client is.

To even ask to review client's financial health can sometimes be a touchy subject. Some firms hold so tight they want to email directly to the ownership instead of having their financials forwarded among brokerage houses. It is your job to educate clients immediately that financials are a large part of the negotiations, as building owners enjoy very strong financials. So make sure your clients are very aware to include their financials with the offer. It also doubles as a strong professional move and shows serious focus on the subject property.

Also owners and sellers are just as busy today and mainly interested in making sure they are working with a viable new prospect. They want to see significant equity, cash flows, and healthy operations and little to no debt. The ownership is determining if this tenant will be around in three to five years seeing they might not be able to speak with the tenant's current landlord.

The top four most requested documents are the Last two years tax returns, current year's profit and loss statements, balance sheet and income statement. If debt documents, credit documents, and a business plan are available, be sure to advise the client to have them at the ready. They may or may not be requested. The goal as always is to spoil the owner to the point they know you are real and well off to make this a success.

If the client financials are subpar or this is a startup company the most likely outcome is a doubling or tripling of security deposit, personal guarantee or letter of credit, on tenant improvements, commissions, and free rent given. So for example, on a five year lease the personal guarantee may burn off, subject to good payment history, but a late payment can trigger the personal guarantee to remain through the entire term.

22.   Office Space Plans and the Recession

After a company has gone through the disposition of surplus space and aligned these metrics to acceptable levels based on their new employee count, what is next?

Improving Space Utilization

Numerous industry studies have shown that the average maximum utilization rate throughout the day for most office space is just 48 percent. A great deal has been written lately about the design of workspace and how companies are looking to do more with less office space. While this trend in some industries began prior to the latest economic downturn, the recession has caused companies to take a more aggressive posture towards office space density.

Office density is defined as the space (per square foot) per workstation. Office density excludes accounting for support spaces and is calculated on a net rentable basis. A higher office density means a lower space per workstation and a lower density means more space per workstation. Measuring office density helps to identify a benchmark for office efficiency in addition to assist with monitoring new office space use techniques.

Workplace Trends

The general trend of the open plan workplace, where managers give up their private offices and join their employees in a more open office environment is becoming more commonplace. Open plan environments have grown in adoption partly due to the perceived cost saving, increased flexibility and the premise this strategy enhances team collaboration, productivity and communication.

Big Four professional services firm Deloitte is starting the build-out of its new 166,000-square-foot San Francisco headquarters and expects to expand the 1,500 person San Francisco office by 10 percent in the next year, the new office will represent a 42 percent decline in square footage from the 285,000 square feet the firm currently occupies.

There is no one size fits all when it comes to office space. How a company utilizes office space is driven by the activities of the organization. For example, Law firms typically have a higher ratio of private offices than other industries. In Houston, the energy capital of the world, we saw many companies in the oil gas sector take the open office space approach and while some have retained that strategy, others have trended back to a more traditional office layout with private offices for senior managers. I would note for energy companies, real estate occupancy costs as a percentage of revenues is much lower than most industries. Whatever strategy a company takes in regards to its office space design, calculating "office density" is the workspace metric that is now in vogue.

23.   Financial Analysis for Office Lease Transactions

Financial Analysis is defined as the set of principles, procedures and tools that help organize and interpret financial data. Making informed real estate decision requires utilizing economic models designed to improve the quality of the lease or facility decision. More than just a software program, this analysis is the product of formal training in finance combined with years of experience in the commercial real estate marketplace.

The decision to renew a lease or relocate your office facilities requires thorough financial analysis of the anticipated lease costs within the marketplace. This requires the technical ability to analyze the cost associated with various facility decisions. To assist in the decision making process it is prudent to compare "Occupancy Costs" of various alternatives in an "apples to apples" format. This approach is important because what often appears to be the most economical deal on the surface in reality may not be the best alternative after evaluating all economic components of the proposed transaction. Although the concept of leasing office space is simple, commercial leases have an increasingly complex financial structure. How does a tenant go about determining the true cost of such a lease? A typical office building lease may include the following:

- Base Rental Payments (fixed or escalated)

- Additional rent provisions for increases in operating expenses

- Caps or ceilings on operating expense escalations

- Periods of abated or reduced rent

- Contributions (loans) by the landlord for leasehold improvements, architectural fees, IT cabling, moving expenses, leasing commissions and existing lease obligations

- Parking charges

- Various options (renewal, expansion, contraction and cancellation)

- Electrical Capacity (watts per square foot) and H.V.A.C. charges

- Add on Factors (Rentable vs. Usable Square Feet)

- Costs to comply with government regulations (ADA)

- Fees for Construction Management

- Interest fees for above standard leasehold improvements

Comparing Occupancy Costs

Once occupancy costs associated with various lease alternatives are identified and the underlying economics of the proposed lease transaction are understood, the projection of the total occupancy costs over the term of the lease and on an annual basis is calculated. These projected annual cash flows are subjected to discounted cash flow analysis (net present value) at an appropriate discount rate (cost of capital) to account for the time value of money. The results are the Net Present Value or "the price of the deal". To clarify for comparison purposes, I express the discounted present value of the lease as a level rate per square foot which enables the tenant to measure the financial structure of the lease proposals on an "apples to apples" basis. The impact of income taxes can be accounted for by discounting cash flows at a rate reflective of the tenant's after tax cost of debt. When comparing alternatives, occupancy cost levels both absolute and present value basis are analyzed in terms of rentable and usable square feet to account for differences in common area factors and space efficiency. The result is the "effective occupancy cost per square foot" which provides a meaningful comparison of various lease proposals.

Today, technology provides us with the software to easily implement the financial analysis of lease transactions. Popular programs include Lease Matrix, REI Wise, ProCalc and Costar Lease Analysis. I learned how to analyze a deal with a HP-12C calculator, which kind of gives away my age. However, it is important to understand the principles of this analysis and how various cash flows impact the overall cost particularly when it comes to the art of negotiation.

Financial Analysis as a Negotiation Tool

Effective negotiations require a thorough understanding of the underlying economics of the transaction. I believe great deals are not only found but also negotiated. My financial skill allows me to measure the impact of various economic components on the value of the lease and to quantify the landlord's effective rental rate. In essence, the landlord's effective rental rate is the net profit level from the lease before the building's debt payments expressed on a square foot basis. By viewing the lease from the landlord's perspective it is relatively simple to benchmark the landlord's projected return and measure the impact of various changes in financial components of the lease on the landlord's bottom line. While comparing rental rates and negotiated concessions to other transactions in the market is an excellent indicator of achievable terms the landlord's effective rate is where the "rubber meets the road". No two lease transactions even with identical rental rates yield the same return to the landlord. My objective is structure a "win – win" transaction while not leaving any money on the negotiation table. Evaluating the landlord's effective rate during negotiations is a key tool in determining the landlord's bottom line.

24. Financial Analysis for Lease Negotiating Tool

Net Effective Rents - "Where the Rubber Meets the Road"

Effective negotiations for an office lease require a thorough understanding of the underlying economics of the transaction. Great deals are not only found, but also negotiated. There are several factors that can impact the terms an office tenant and his broker can negotiate such as:

- The Tenant's attractiveness to the Landlord and negotiation leverage

- Size and creditworthiness of the Tenant

- Market conditions and the buildings position within the marketplace

- Timing and positioning of the negotiations

- The overall negotiation skills of the participants involved

Having the financial skills to measure the impact of various economic components on the value of the lease and to quantify the landlord's effective rental rate is a valuable tool.

By viewing the lease from the landlord's perspective it is relatively simple to benchmark the landlord's projected return and measure the impact of various changes in financial components of the lease on the landlord's bottom line. In essence, the landlord's "effective rental rate" is the net profit level from the lease before the building's debt payments expressed on a square foot basis.

The Anatomy of the Effective Rental Rate

Understanding how a landlord proforma's his building is important. They have to project their effective rental rates. This is what is left over to service the debt on the building and provide a return to the building investors. To determine their projected effective rent structure they look at:

- Market Rental Rates for Comparable Buildings: What can they charge?

- Operating Costs: What does it cost to operate the building?

- Transaction Costs: Tenant Improvements, Commissions, Free rent

In simple terms, it is a calculation of all the projected in-flows and outflows of cash from leasing and operations. They do project vacancy periods for unoccupied space, but they basically are targeting an effective rent structure that forms a basis for leasing decisions. For illustration purposes, search online for online calculation of the Landlord's net effective rent to stay updated on all moving factors in ownership calculations.

25. Renewal Option

Who Benefits from a Renewal Option? Most commercial office leases are long-term in nature, typically 5, 7 or 10 years in length, but also typically contain provisions for extending the lease beyond the initial term. A renewal clause in a real estate lease allows a tenant to decide whether or not to extend the lease once the initial lease term expires. The key concept to remember is that the renewal option is a benefit to the Tenant.

Short-Term versus Long-Term Leases

A quick on-line search of articles written on the subject of the renewal option shows in most cases, these articles emphasized the point that Landlords and commercial leasing agents typically want tenants to sign long-term leases and the better approach was to sign shorter term leases with renewal options. In some cases a shorter term lease may be a more prudent strategy for a company; however there are disadvantages to signing short-term leases including:

- Short-term leases equate to less negotiation leverage and fewer concessions.

- Tenant improvement allowance: If you need significant improvements to renovate the space to your needs then expect to come out of pocket for the costs. The shorter the lease term, the less the Landlord is going to provide in funds for tenant improvements.

- The inability to fix rental costs for a longer period and exposure to higher rental rates in subsequent renewal terms.

Most of the authors of these articles recommended asking for renewal options with predetermined increases for a series of renewal options. This sounds great in theory, if you can get the Landlord to agree to what you consider reasonable predetermined rent increases. However, the reality is very few Landlords are willing to give you that flexibility without paying a premium, even in a soft market. In other words, expect those predetermined increases to be rather significant.

The whole short-term versus long-term lease decision comes to down to flexibility and what's the cost associated with that flexibility. There are reasons businesses sign longer term leases and short-term leases are the exception rather than the rule. Generally speaking longer term leases result in lower costs. More flexibility is sometimes necessary and the additional cost or limitations associated with short-term leases is worth the trade-off.

Negotiating a Favorable Renewal Option

Landlords reluctantly grant renewal options because it limits their flexibility to market the space to prospective tenants. However, they typically recognize it's going to be required in order to complete a lease transaction with most tenants. The "Renewal Clause" spells out when the tenant is required to exercise their renewal option, the term of the renewal period and the rental amount and/or the method for determining the financial terms for the renewal period.

Elements of the Renewal Option:

Notice Period: Most renewal clauses require the tenant to give written notice to the Landlord that they are exercising their right to the renewal option within a specified period of time, often 6 or 12 months prior to the expiration of the lease. From the Tenant's perspective you want to make this notice period as long and as flexible as possible, giving you and your broker time to thoroughly evaluate the market, solicit proposals from competitive buildings and make a good business decision while your option period is in effect.

Term: The renewal clause will state the length of the lease renewal period. If possible when negotiating the renewal clause, ask for the option to renew the lease with different length terms (i.e. 3/5 years or 5/10 years).

Rental Rate: In some cases the renewal clause will have a predetermined renewal rental rate, but the more common approach is to have the renewal financial terms tied to a determination of "fair market value" (FMV).

Fair Market Value: It is important to define in detail the definition of "fair market value" because in essence, this is a negotiation that will take place at a later date. The objective is to leave as little as possible subject to the Landlord's interpretation of FMV. Does the definition of FMV include accounting for tenant improvement allowances, free rent, and other concessions offered by competitive buildings? Is there a floor for the minimum rent? I have often seen language in the clause that states; "in no event shall the tenant pay less than the current rental amount" Can you get a ceiling on the maximum rent; 95% of FMV? What if the Landlord and Tenant cannot agree on FMV? The renewal clause should also contain a mechanism for engaging a third party arbitrator if the two parties cannot agree to terms.

The Renewal Option Protects the Tenant

In reality, the renewal option provides very little if any benefit to the Landlord. For the tenant it is important because it can protect their rights and negotiation leverage in market conditions or a situation that is tilted in the Landlord's favor.

• Another tenant may be willing to pay a higher rental rate than you for your current space.

• A larger tenant in the building may want your space for expansion.

• You may have made a huge financial investment in improvements or infrastructure in your space and the Landlord knows it will be cost prohibitive to move.

If you have a well structured renewal option, it acts as the framework for putting a ceiling on the costs of renewing the lease for your office space. In a soft, tenant-oriented market the renewal option is not as critical. The Landlord wants to you to renew at the best terms they can achieve, but realizes competition for your tenancy and market conditions will prevent them from invoking any predetermined framework outlined in the renewal option.

When you are negotiating your lease it is difficult to predict what business and market conditions will look like 5 or 10 years down the road. If you do not have a renewal option in your lease or it is poorly structured, it could be very costly. However, a well structured renewal option can save you a significant amount of money, particularly in a tight market.

The renewal option may seem secondary to the primary lease terms that are important to your business today. However, down the road the renewal option can have a big impact on your business. It is important to assume that market conditions are going to be in the Landlord's favor when it becomes time to exercise the renewal option.

26. CRM or Customer Relationship Management Platforms

CRM or Customer Relationship Management Platforms are software programs to manage a broker or brokerage firm's encounters with clients, vendors, and servicers, with an extremely time focused automation. CRM is one of the most vital areas to focus on throughout your career to help yourself, team, company and most of all clients. Always work on updating, upgrading, and testing new management tools as technology is the path to success in real estate today.

With CRM you are almost creating work for a full time electronic assistant that updates you on who to call at what time and what the conversation was about previously. Other benefits include, mass mailers either physical mail or email, lease expirations, annual increase time frames, auto updates for important business related functions. Lastly mobile access is the key today as well as pulling up lock box codes for each property and details of each product suite. CRM for commercial real estate is absolutely essential to most.

Below are some of the best examples you can find on the internet today. One of the most productive ways is to ask other tenant reps in forums, your office, your colleagues, and ask these CRM firms for recommendations in your specific market and product type. Most, if not all, have training courses and continuous education is essential.

Apto

Bpm'online

ClientLook

RealNex

RealHound

HighTower

PowerBroker

REthink

Here are some not focused on Commercial Real Estate but are noteworthy

SalesForce

Insightly

Highrise

Great Tenant Representation Tools

LeaseMatrix

ProCalc

planEASe

27.   Leveraging the Internet

Today, many colleagues and peers will likely not argue that digital strategies are important tools in marketing both commercial property and real estate services, but to date there has not been a ton of data to clearly understand the role the internet plays in commercial real estate.

Google Inc and LoopNet recently released the results of a joint study you can find online if you Google: "Commercial Real Estate Consumer Online Behavior and Trends". The study, which aimed to understand the role the internet plays in commercial real estate, leverages Google's proprietary online search data and custom research conducted on LoopNet's behalf by Market Connections, an independent research firm, in 2014 to survey and analyze the behaviors of tenants and investors currently involved in a commercial property search and who have recently been involved in a transaction.

Some key findings from the study:

1) 80% of tenants and investors surveyed agree that they rely on the internet for their commercial real estate information needs more now than three years ago.
2) Over three quarters (78%) of tenants and investors surveyed use online commercial real estate services or tools at some point in their commercial real estate search.
3) Commercial real estate related online searches have grown 60% since 2008.
4) Six in 10 respondents search for commercial properties using their mobile devices at least sometimes.
5) Over half the survey respondents (55%) reported that they perform their own online searches for commercial property, even when they are working with a broker.

What does this all mean and how do we benefit? Get involved in internet platforms before you finish reading this book. Below are companies you need to work with now.

theBrokerList
OfficeSpace
ROFO
OfficeFinder
LoopNet
Regus
RealFacilities
ITRAGlobal
CompStak
TheSquareFoot
RealMassive
42Floors
OfficeLocator

Lastly subscribe and follow Coy Davidson, you can build a following and leverage the internet for referrals in your own market or submarket or zip code by leveraging Coy.

28.   Managing Account Relationships

Managing the tenant's expectations is an art and science. After the initial lease or purchase occupancy, you must routinely check in and take action on items that are obvious and not obvious to the client. Obvious items are annual rental increases, the exact months they receive free rent, when their pre payment of rent burns off, and the time frames when to renegotiate a renewal typically 9 months before expiration. Non Obvious are growing pains, sublease issues, impossible landlord issues, new energy efficiency issues, or blend and extend issues.

Typically across the board checking in roughly 90-180 days with the decision maker will ensure that the decision maker understands you are very available to help with any time critical issue. Not only do you position yourself as available, as an expert, but you are also the company's unofficial in-house real estate department without being on their books or a cost to their time and dollar. Ensuring expertise and being available to the client without a cost to their company needs to be advertised to earn your place in their company.

29.   Vendor List for the Client

The excitement of landing an amazing deal for the client and getting to the end of signing the lease, cutting the rental checks and providing insurance is not the finish line, but very close. Tenants need assistance before, during, and after a lease signing. Here is a list of the typical vendors a tenant would need to have in your market.   The goal is to have immediate access, via a branded document, you share and provide for your clients at a seconds notice outlining the various resources they may need. You should also be the tenant rep for these vendor companies or have a strong connection so you can show a tight relationship with all inner circles. This is your network and needs to be constantly growing so you act as a connector to all companies you refer.

Insurance -

Legal Services -

Moving and Storage Specialist -

Project Manager -

General Contractor -

Architect -

Interior decorator –

Printing and Signage-

Water, Coffee, and Drink Services -

Office Furniture (Cubicles, Desks, Cabinets, Filing, Reception) –

Office Supply (Copiers, Printers, Mailers, Drones) -

IT/Telephone (Wi-Fi, WI-Max, Cabling, Server, Digital, 3D) –

Security Products-

Janitor and waste management -

Residential Relocation Specialist –

Office Shredding -

Event (Party) Planner -

30.   Move and or Relocation Services

If you work with a client that has multiple locations in multiple cities and states, moving and occupancy will be one of the largest struggles out of the services list you provide. To reduce the tenant's stress of planning, down times, and logistics, help eliminate this stress to create a favorable outcome by insuring you have a number of procedures in place.

Interview at least 3 moving companies that are in the zip code the tenant is moving to or currently in. Immediately ask for trade references, proof of insurance coverage, and what the ball park pricing is for your type of client, employee head count, and distance. More information will be needed for a concrete number but the starting point will set the stage if this moving company is prequalified and not a fly by night or start up moving enterprise.

Put an excel sheet together of the companies that are motivated to help the client and work to finalize the pricing. Over time you will have built up a large list of moving companies for specific markets which will be a benefit too. In large institutional quality assets the property manager onsite can provide a list of vendor servicers that are approved for their project and have had experience moving tenants.

31.   5 Things CEO's Want from their Commercial Real Estate Space

Objectives for a New Office Space

Some of my best blog posts are often simple and summarize real conversations with real clients. Just this week I sat down with the CEO of a NYSE publicly traded company who has retained me to assist in identifying and securing a new location for their corporate headquarters. While we discussed many important location and building selection criteria. I asked him to summarize his key objectives in securing new office space for their corporate headquarters.

I want our new office space to:

Reflect the proper, as well as a positive image on the company to clients, investors, partners and employees.

Enhance our ability to attract and retain key talent.

Demonstrate to our employees we are concerned about their health and wellbeing, (i.e. natural light, amenities and security).

Be designed to enhance collaboration and enhance operational efficiency.

Be impressive, yet not overly lavish (i.e. cost effective).

32.   Commissions

The Truth about Leasing Commissions

One of the discussions many commercial real estate agents don't like to have with their prospective clients revolves around the subject of fees or commissions. I have often seen brokers in an attempt to secure representation agreements with tenants, make the claim that their services are free. This is a play on words, what they should be saying is; "the Landlord makes the actual fee payment and you are not required to make a direct payment for my services".

The Money Has to Come from Somewhere

If currency changes hands, it is not free! I believe that it is important that the scope of services to be provided by a brokerage firm and the fees associated with these services should be clearly defined with the prospective client.

In the office leasing arena, it is typical that the broker(s) both the Landlord's and the Tenant's representative are paid a fee after the lease is executed between the Landlord and the Tenant. The fact is most costs associated with the lease transaction including the leasing commissions are rolled into the final negotiated terms and paid back to the landlord in the form of rent over the term of the lease, including both the Tenant and Landlord agent's commission. Building owners typically budget real estate commissions into their pro-forma and any commission that is not paid rarely finds its way back into the tenant's pocket.

Leasing commissions are not set and are always negotiable, but generally speaking in the Houston office market, the tenant representative will request a four percent (4%) fee of the gross lease value paid by the Landlord the Tenant contracts with. Also, in most cases the Landlord's agent will receive two percent (2%) of the gross lease value, paid also by the Landlord for leasing his property. Some cities have slightly different percentages or payment arrangements that are typical for that market, but for the most part, this is the general cost of the services provided.

I would argue that in theory, the tenant is not only paying for his broker's services but also the Landlord's agent's services, which only reinforces the fact; that tenants should have professional representation. In most leasing arrangements brokers have with building owners, if the leasing agent completes a transaction directly with a tenant who does not have representation, they get a bigger fee (4%). So under this scenario, the net cost of the tenant representative is 2% of the gross lease value. A good tenant representative's services will save you five times this amount or more in occupancy cost over the term of your lease if not much more, in many cases. So the next time, a commercial real estate agent tells you his services are "free" I suggest finding a new one to consider to represent your company.

"A commercial real estate professional will clearly outline not only his scope of services, but what their fee is, how they get paid and where the money comes from."

33.   Build to Suit Office Space

Why Consider a Build to Suit Office Lease?

In order for a business to satisfy its office space requirements they have basically four options:

1.   Lease or sublease vacant office space;

2.   Acquire an existing building and renovate;

3.   Build and own your own facility; or

4.   A build to suit to lease.

The Build to Suit Lease

A build to suit lease is an alternative that allows the user/tenant to design and customize a new facility to meet the enterprise's unique space needs without the large up-front capital expenditure that comes with building and owning. In a build to suit to lease arrangement, a company selects a real estate developer to design and build a customized facility on a preferred site and then leases it from the developer. Under this structure, the user never owns the facility.

A build to suit lease can offer several advantages to the company whose current space no longer ideally meets their objectives. It allows the tenant to expand the realm of optimal location choices and maximum space efficiency, since the facility is designed specifically for the tenant. New construction allows a developer to incorporate the most recent cost-effective energy systems in the project, incorporate state of the art technology and construction materials with the goal of operating efficiency. The building can be designed to project the company's image, attract and retain employees as well as enhance productivity and logistics. These key objectives can sometimes be challenging in varying degrees, when leasing or renovating an existing facility.

Long Term Lease Solution

A build to suit lease is not a short-term office space solution. A long-term office lease commitment is necessary for the developer / owner to acquire financing and the tenant's creditworthiness must be acceptable to lenders to obtain favorable financing terms. The build-to-suit process is lengthy and may take several years to complete. Once the build-to-suit decision is made and a developer/owner is selected; a transaction has to be finalized which is inherently more complicated since there is a lease and complex construction component beyond your typical office build-out. In addition, the preferred land site has to be acquired and the building has to be designed and built.

Evaluating All Your Options

A build to suit lease is generally considered more expensive than leasing existing office space, particularly in today's market where office vacancy rates have risen and building owners are aggressively courting office tenants with attractive lease terms and concessions. However, the difference may be offset in the long-term by savings in office space efficiency, reduced operating costs and improved company image.

When considering new construction, particularly for very large corporations, the user may have better borrowing power or a lower cost of capital than the developer. So it would seem owning the building your office would be more cost effective. However, for most companies real estate is not their core business and they choose to allocate their investment capital to other strategic operating initiatives that offer a higher rate of return on their investment.

For every company each of the four office space occupancy strategies has its own merits and disadvantages. A prudent business owner or management team will evaluate each option with their real estate advisors to determine which alternative best suits their needs. In some cases some of these options may not be a realistic or viable strategy. However, for the company desiring an office building designed specifically for their unique needs, the build to suit offers a new, customized facility without the significant capital expenditure of building and owning your office space.

34.   Office Space Density: The New Workspace Metric

With the advances in technology in the work world and recessionary periods there is going to be an increasing focus on cost control and efficiency. One of the first places companies look to reduce cost is to examine their real estate, which is typically one of their largest expenses, second only to staffing. The quickest and most significant way to reduce real estate costs is to eliminate space.

Step one to improving space utilization is typically to eliminate surplus space through subleasing, lease terminations, consolidating locations and selling non-productive real estate assets. Historically occupancy costs have been benchmarked in terms of three primary metrics:

- Square feet per employee

- Occupancy costs as a percentage of sales or revenues

- Occupancy cost per employee

Numerous industry studies have shown that the average maximum utilization rate throughout the day for most office space is just 48 percent. A great deal has been written lately about the design of workspace and how companies are looking to do more with less office space. While this trend in some industries began prior to the latest economic downturn, the recession has caused companies to take a more aggressive posture towards office space density.

Office density is defined as the space (per square foot) per workstation. Office density excludes accounting for support spaces and is calculated on a net rentable basis. A higher office density means a lower space per workstation and a lower density means more space per workstation. Measuring office density helps to identify a benchmark for office efficiency in addition to assist with monitoring new office use techniques.

<u>Workplace Trends</u>

The general trend of the open plan workplace, where managers give up their private offices and join their employees in a more open office environment is becoming more commonplace. Open plan environments have grown in adoption partly due to the perceived cost saving, increased flexibility and the premise that this strategy enhances team collaboration, productivity and communication. There is no one size fits all when it comes to office space. How a company utilizes office space is driven by the activities of the organization. Whatever strategy a company takes in regards to its office space design, calculating "office density" is the workspace metric that is now in vogue.

35.   Rent to Revenue Ratio

Most companies use a few basic metrics when comparing various office locations from a transactional standpoint or attempting to benchmark the performance of various operating properties across their real estate portfolio. The three most utilized measures are:

1. Cost per square foot
2. Square feet per person
3. Occupancy cost per person

The Rent to Revenue Ratio

Today, a measure that is becoming increasingly utilized by many corporate real estate executives and savvy service providers is the rent-to-revenue ratio. Most industries, geographic regions and local economies have benchmarked rent-to-revenue ratios, or in simple terms, the percentage of sales that you should be allocating toward property that is typical for your specific industry. Standard rent-to-revenue ratios can vary from as little as 2% in some industries to as high as 15% for some professional service organizations such as law firms.

The logic behind utilizing this metric is to enhance the ability to make strategic decisions about the appropriate level of investment in your workspace for various locations and if a particular location or workspace strategy justifies the higher expense associated with it, it will clearly be evident in the increase in revenue generation associated with that decision.

Historically companies have always focused the spotlight on projecting the cost side of the equation when making real estate decisions particularly from a transactional standpoint. Business decisions are sometimes made whereby the full implications of the real estate component are not given primary consideration. In an expanding economy where most companies are experiencing solid revenue growth there is a larger margin for error when occupancy costs are not aligned properly with revenue levels, and it's not until there is a negative disruption in revenue that the implication of the decision become painful.

More and more emphasis is being placed on expenses as a percent of revenue as companies increasingly look at corporate real estate as a tool to gain a competitive advantage. Calculating rent to revenue ratios shifts the spotlight beyond just occupancy costs to the bottom line and will serve as a tool for better real estate decisions.

36. Buy vs Lease

When is the Right Time to Buy Your Office Space Instead of Lease It?

This is a question I have heard many times from clients over my 20 year career, typically when lease rates are at historical highs or property values drop and begin to look attractive. I think without question that recent economic and real estate market conditions have created opportunities for corporate users to acquire properties for their operational use with attractive financial terms.

The idea of owning your business real estate for companies who never have seems like a great idea. For major corporate users with multiple locations who typically both lease and own key facilities there is less emotional appeal, and it is strictly a financial decision as they understand the implications of owning real estate and whether it's a viable operational choice for a particular space requirement.

Most companies are in the real estate business by default as it serves as an operational need to produce products or provide services. The decision to buy versus lease corporate real estate is not a consideration that should be based solely on the financial considerations but should include evaluation of a more comprehensive set of decision drivers. Corporate real estate decisions are not only about the financial implications but also managing the risk associated with that decision.

Many internal and external factors affect such decisions and their eventual outcomes. These factors have to be carefully evaluated in order to make the decision that best compliments the overall business objectives of your organization.

Why Today Might be the Right Time to Own

These items address the financial implications of the decision:

Lower Real Estate Values

Office buildings and industrial property prices have dropped across the board and very significantly in many markets. While we are beginning to see a fairly strong rebound in values in some markets, this trend has been confined to trophy properties in key markets. According to the Moody's/REAL Commercial Property Price Index (CPPI), prices have fallen to the levels of 2003/2004 and for some markets and asset classes the value deterioration may not be over for another 12 to 18 months.

Low Borrowing Costs

The cost of debt to acquire real estate is at historical lows particularly for the owner occupant. Access to cheap funds available to financially sound corporate users is going to make ownership look very enticing and the delta between their cost to borrow compared to real-estate-investors' cost to borrow is significant.

Cash Surpluses

Corporate earnings have been solid and many companies survived the recession sitting on significant cash reserves. U.S. companies are holding a record nearly $2 trillion in cash according to the Federal Reserve Bank and have been hesitant to hire again, but once they start they have the surplus capital necessary to invest in real estate without impacting other capital investment objectives.

Lease Accounting

The proposed lease accounting changes will place all leases onto the balance sheet, taking away one of the benefits of leasing (at least for those companies who have been sensitive to how much assets are on their balance sheet).

Weighing the Benefits and the Risks

However as I have alluded to, an attractive financial transaction does not always translate into the best real estate decision. The benefits and risks of each option have to be weighed carefully.

Leasing Benefits

- Lower up front capital requirements
- The availability of various lease term choices (length) that best fit your companies projected operational requirements
- More flexibility for growth and contraction both short and long term
- Ease of disposition at the end of the lease term

Leasing Risks

- Exposure to fluctuations in market rents and landlord-provided concession packages and incentives
- Potential for missed option and notice dates
- Disposition prior to end-of-term can be challenging, depending on market conditions and other factors
- Typically dependent on third-party property management and service providers for quality of life and service issues
- Building ownership can change hands

Ownership Benefits

- Property Value Appreciation
- At some point with continued occupancy, ownership becomes less expensive each year on an actual cash basis
- Realization of residual value of tenant improvement costs
- Depreciation for some entities
- Tax Benefits (Income and Property if municipality offers incentives)
- Control of quality of life and property management vendors

- Ownership of real estate is a separate non-core business that requires time, real estate expertise and resources
- Less flexibility than leasing particularly in growth and contraction
- Potential loss in asset value
- Economic and Interest rate risk
- Risk associated with change in demographics, transportation issues, and perceived neighborhood quality

Decision Drivers

1. Required capital outlay (including retrofit costs)
2. Required return on investment
3. Internal competition for capital
4. Short vs. long-term plans impacted by other large capital investment initiatives
5. Projection of required employee headcount based on revenue, product or service demand (static or rapid changes)
6. Projected market conditions
7. Demographic and labor force shifts
8. Neighborhood stability
9. Capital appreciation
10. Income tax implications
11. Financial reporting
12. Perception of stability as a result of ownership
13. Exit strategy

The buy versus lease decision has a myriad of financial and operational factors that extend beyond the real estate asset and its projected occupancy cost. There should be equally as much consideration given to business needs and expectations. The recent depreciation of property values as a result of the recession also is evident in lease rates. Today's market creates the opportunity for the commercial space user to take advantage and either purchase or lock into long term leases at bargain terms compared to peak market levels prior to the recession. Lease rates will change as the economy recovers, concession packages will get leaner and market rents will eventually escalate. You can effectively achieve long-term control of a facility with a 7-15 years lease commitment and build flexibility into a long term lease with expansion, contraction and renewal options, but there will likely be some scheduled rent increases or exposure to appreciation of market rents.

Owning is Typically More Advantageous as a Long Term Decision, Keep the End in Mind

Purchasing a facility can certainly be a prudent long-term occupancy decision with significant financial reward and operational advantages. The real question in my mind assuming the economics are attractive is how much or how likely will your business or space requirement change, and will owning a building create significant challenges in managing those changes? Owning versus buying is not only a financial decision but equally as much a risk and operational decision.

You have to consider not only how attractive ownership might be going in, but also what will be different if you own and how you will meet unexpected changing space needs. Can the building or site be expanded or is leasing additional space at nearby buildings viable. Is excess space marketable to third party tenants if staff reductions are necessary, and what is the exit strategy and projected value of the asset if required to sell.

37.   Leasing Office Space

Out of all the product categories tenant representation networks work in, office space is the most widely talked about and focused on. Office tenants typically relocate every 3-10 years or on average every 5 years. Office space tenants move for multiple reasons such as contraction, expansion, technologies, key employee hires, and some market trends such as moving employees to new spaces to create renewed enthusiasm and moral with employees for the opportunity to increase productivity.

Office space decisions can come with a lot of decisions. Size, price, location, view, central local to all management and key employees, near certain amenities such as retail and eateries, data centers, other competition or non competing entities, complimentary companies, etc. Some office tenant reps even focus solely on tech firms or law firms because of the expertise that is needed with length of term, size, growth initiatives, creative or professional office look, etc.

Office Users tend to sign office space leases with longer terms than industrial users but less than medical and retail users, which puts them in the marketplace less often. One of the first decisions they should understand is to retain a broker with experience in leasing office space,

Three key issues for a laser focused office tenant rep include:

1.   Employee count. The amount of cold callers to private office needs is three to four times in square foot difference. Understand the employee mix and you can nail the amount of office square feet needed.

2.   Tech or non Tech: You will need to know if a tenant needs fiber optic cable, dedicated single pass air server closet, high utilities barriers, and items such as deck to deck walls for security purposes. Know your niche and this will become common questions and answers with clients, not to mention it could be new insight to tell prospective tenants. Keyless cell phone entry, for example was a common requirement in 2015.

3.   Tenant Improvements and Term: The cost of build-out for the typical office user is $15-$60 per square foot depending on Class C, B or A office finishes. The higher the class of building, such as class A the lease term increases as building ownership will be bearing the higher finish costs to build offices, reception, break room, IT server closet, etc. For example a five year commitment at $2.00 SF with some free rent will equate to roughly $40 SF or roughly 24 months of negative rent for the owner which is why a five year is needed.

38.   Leasing Industrial Space

Leasing Industrial Space means leasing property that serves purposes of storage, warehousing, light and heavy manufacturing, food preparation and cold storage, distribution, from healthy to hazardous materials. Leasing Industrial space harbors knowledge not only on type and size but also what areas the city allows the type of warehousing needs such as hazardous storage or what is being emitted when manufactured. Industrial space is characterized as having low employee head count and a resulting reduced parking requirement, typically one parking space per thousand square feet.

Industrial or warehouse users typically grow by demand and supply of their products much differently than office where most products with office spaces are digital where Industrial and warehouse is physical or material. Size and length of term becomes very critical when supply and demand comes into play. This is where a typical lease for a company is in the twelve to sixty month range if there are no options for immediate expansion into adjacent suites.

When leasing industrial space the most common decisions are location, size, and price, with emphasis on ceiling height, the amount of grade and dock high doors, power and utility requirements or minimums, as well as office to warehouse mix.

Some of these key issues for a laser focused industrial tenant rep include:

1.   Products: Find out exactly what will be be stored, distributed or manufactured to make sure the client is in compliance with zoning , City laws, Health Codes, proximity to citizens, schools, and other companies for the health and welfare of other surrounding entities. Use issues can become a deal killer instantly so know your market requirements immediately seeing they will change from time to time, and area to area.

2.   Size and Ceiling Height: Size comes into play as many firms look for both the ideal square foot as well as an ideal cubic foot location. Cubic Feet encompass the height of the warehouse and storage companies can benefit from high ceiling warehouses where racking of goods can go up three to ten racks high.

3.   Tenant Improvements and Term: The cost of build-out for the typical Industrial space is mainly focused on the small office portion and is typically paint and carpet. Rental rates for industrial are the lowest in commercial real estate which is great for the bottom dollar but tenant improvement dollars are limited since the pay back is two to three times as long as an office space build out. If a firm has their growth projections correct for the next five years tenant improvements can become available but most landlords just provide limited tenant improvements or a rental abatement in the form of months free or many months of half rent. Companies that just need 1,000-5,000 SF expansion space quickly tend to just take spaces on an "as-is" basis on short twelve to twenty four month leases to satisfy unexpected growth until it becomes expected.

4.   Utilities and Amenities: Some deal points that are often overlooked and can become deal killers are power requirements or minimum power requirements, sprinkler requirements, water requirements, yard storage requirements, as well as the number and size grade level and dock high loading doors. The more you find out what your client needs bare minimum the easier it will become to find that new location. For future plays remember which owners have solar to provide tenants that have large power

needs which can turn into an instant energy saving amenity. In the future multiple listing platforms will have tabs for solar which you will be prepared for by reading this book.

39.   Leasing Flex Space

Leasing Flex Space is typically found in buildings that are built for specific purposes or were originally designed and built for industrial space then converted as needed for more office, biotech lab, clean tech, research and development, and some retailing.

Flex space has more heating, ventilation and air conditioning units on the roof then just generic warehouse space. Generic warehouse space may be 90% warehouse and 10% office. Many flex spaces we see today have been converted industrial buildings where owners take on the risk of converting into specific niche uses. Typically converted flex space buildings have over fifty percent office space built out, the buildings themselves do not have high ceilings roughly under eighteen feet high or less and do not have amenities such as heavy power or transformers.

One of the best examples are the creative office flex spaces that internet and marketing companies enjoy with large open collaborative rooms where a lot of sharing and working together can be achieved. Next is biotech where expansion of very expensive clean room and labs can be built out, and lastly research and development where variables such as climate control and large open ventilated rooms are available.

The main points for knowing Flex space cold is to know the niches.

1) Biotech or Lab Space can be an entire focus for a tenant rep in markets where biotech is king and scientists are readily available. The main factors that come into play are zoning, code compliances, environmental controls, hazardous uses, and the amount of clean room to lab space to hazardous and dangerous storage space to office space. Life Science and pharmaceutical companies rarely are alike which is why it is so critical to consistently ask all the correct questions. Some labs may require over a thousand dollars per square foot in tenant improvements and that can easily make or break a deal if overlooked.

Other factors to consider are what your city has for GMP or Good Manufacturing Practices and clean room standards that will ultimately be reviewed during and after construction by organizations such as the FDA. This is where you need to find out the top three biotech consultants that can help you with any immediate need. Lastly because Biotech is one of the most expensive types of build outs, know the grants and incentives cold for new start ups or clients that are unfamiliar. Being the most knowledgeable about the Biotech Niche will make you a very memorial tenant rep.

2) R&D, High Tech or Clean Tech spaces is another niche to know. Here you have typical industrial building construction where almost the entire industrial building has heating, ventilation, air conditioning, commonly known as HVAC. Here you have standard office and administration features with research, development, production, testing or products and technologies in the rear. Typical clients will request the correct amount of size and office to R&D/Tech ratio, sprinklers, power, special air quality control environments twenty four hours a day, seven days a week. R&D and Tech continue to evolve and so will the unique requirements for layouts.

3) Creative Space as noted previously is another niche in the flex space world. For Creative open office looks more and more these days the open soft and hard wood ceilings with chrome style ducting, stained or epoxy floors and amenities you would remember from the dot com era. One of the major

reasons tenants consider paying a little higher in rent for creative office spaces is to retain or pull in top talent. Today more than ever more people are choosing who and where they want to work and the smart evolving firms understand and act on this. More pleasing to the eye environments can create more favorable employees and higher moral. Some Creative spaces have lounges, yoga studios, relaxation, and think tank rooms. This is where companies have employees that work almost around the clock and need to have a pleasing environment to really gain on a day's work.

4) Budget Office Space is another advantage to a firm that wants to save as much they can on rental expenses or have situations such as thin margin operations. Here the industrial building is converted to office space typically with a large open portion for cubicle work environments for call centers, customer service and relation centers and larger than average bathroom stalls and kitchen break rooms. Generators are also a key factor in ensuring a company's success as well as finding converted industrial buildings that have ample parking compared to the normal one parking space per thousand square feet. Otherwise company executives and employees are forced to park on the street because of the low parking ratio.

40.   Leasing Retail Space

Retail spaces come in many shapes, sizes, locations, attributes, and costs. Retail is another very specialized niche in the commercial real estate world so most tenants seek a tenant rep that exclusively focuses on retail. In light of retail most tenant reps lease in strip centers, community centers and power centers. Strip centers are multi tenant locations that have typically two or more retail tenants, anchor or non anchor tenants that share a mix of retail fronts that benefit customers with typical everyday products such as fast food, dry cleaning, nail salons, auto body, flower, and professional services. Urban retail is generally comprised of strip centers or one retail location that is in a central business district, which is the most common example of retail locations in in major cities.

The least recognized retail representation is with Regional malls or super malls typically are handled with much different cost and build out metrics seeing they are unique. Regional malls or super malls are categorized as being over three hundred and fifty thousand feet to four million square feet with multiple anchor tenants with competing uses that occupy twenty five to two hundred thousand square feet of space. In the twenty first century there are roughly fifteen hundred regional malls or super malls and the growth has frozen and has already started on the decline because of the power of shopping online. For example Jet.com is one of the greatest internet startups for membership shopping. Jet.com is one of the fastest and highest capital raise in internet history which charges roughly fifty dollars a year to be able to buy the lowest priced products around the world by linking discounts and specials and products that can offer steep discounts that customers buy on a regular basis. This was never around before and is another huge industry factor that is reducing the retail footprint around the world.

The main points for retail locations are:

1) Location: Location, Location, Location, never assume a location will catch on, make sure every location strategy is definitive and backed by studies, strategies, comps, traffic counts, experience, progress, incentives, etc. Location in retail is everything and legendary. Nail the location and nail the the future of success and expansion.

2) Incentives: Retail has some of the broadest negotiations with rental rate, NNN caps, length of term, free rent, half rent, tenant improvements, signage agreements, percentage rents, escape or out clauses, graduated lease payments, revenue subleasing, etc. Make sure your offerings are overwhelming as landlords in the retail product category enjoy seeing simple offers that leave a lot out.

41.   Leasing Medical Space

Medical office space users and physician practices don't typically relocate to new buildings as often as general office tenants. However, the competition for new patients is increasingly steering physician practices to non-hospital campus properties as they seek more conveniently accessible locations for their patient base.

This trend is evident in the increased development of smaller suburban medical office projects and urgent care clinics you see in any significant metropolitan community. Furthermore it is increasingly common to see healthcare providers take space in smaller community retail centers near hospital campuses.

Medical users also tend to sign office space leases with longer terms than your typical office tenant, which puts them in the marketplace for office space less often. While many of the same sound principles required to lease general office space apply to healthcare, there are many nuances and issues that are unique to medical users that should be considered.

One of the first decisions they should make is to retain a broker with experience in leasing medical office space. Hiring a tenant representative is prudent for any tenant. However, brokers who have experience in leasing medical office space can be particularly helpful because they may be aware of available buildings and space that have not come to the attention of the practice and they understand how to structure terms and covenants of the lease agreement to fit the unique needs of the healthcare provider.

Some of these key issues include:

1.   Use Issues: Medical tenants use hazardous materials and generate biomedical waste. Medical tenants can use X-ray machines, CT scans, and other machines which may generate harmful radiation. As a result this creates special requirements that need to be accounted for in the lease document to ensure compliance.

2.   After Hours Access & Utilities: Medical tenants often may see patients after normal building hours and in the case of urgent care clinics operate on a 24-hour basis. Paying special attention to how the utilities are accounted for after normal building hours can save un-necessary utility expenses.

3.   Compliance with Americans with Disabilities Act (ADA): Patients are more likely than the general public to have special access needs. Buildings containing health care providers are more likely to receive ADA scrutiny. As a practical matter, medical tenants must pay special attention to the ADA clause contained in the lease document.

4.   Landlord Inspection & Privacy: Generally, commercial leases provide the landlord the right to re-enter your space to show the premises to future tenants, inspect for compliance with the lease and allow access to make infrastructure repairs in the lease premises and elsewhere in the building. Yet health care providers need to limit the landlord's access to examining rooms and other areas during certain hours of the day as well as non-access to patient records.

5.   Anti Kick-back Issues: Safe harbors created under the Federal anti-kickback laws create special requirements for leases between medical tenants and properties that are hospital or physician owned. Proper compliance and documentation must be addressed if that type of landlord-tenant relationship exists.

6.   Exclusivity Provisions: An exclusive use provision is a lease term in which the landlord promises not to lease any other space in the development to a party whose intended use would be in direct competition with tenant's use of its space. In medical office buildings it can be prudent to get exclusivity for your specific specialty practice.

7.   Death & Disability Clauses: In the case of solo practitioners, the concept of getting a death and disability clause in the lease providing for the ability to cancel the lease (typically with penalty) in the event the physician is unable to practice due to death or disability should be explored. Landlords will resist with the argument that the tenants insurance should provide for this, but in some cases, this provision can be successfully negotiated into lease agreements.

8.   Tenant Improvements: The cost of build-out for the typical medical user often greatly exceeds that of a general office tenant. In today's market even a modest office design can run $40.00-$60.00 per square foot. The extensive plumbing, millwork and equipment compliance issue creates additional cost as well as specific lease and transaction issues, including:

-     Term: As a result of the typically higher tenant finish out costs it common for medical office leases to be 7-10 years in term as opposed to 3-5 years for general office tenants. The longer term should result in a larger tenant improvement allowance for the Landlord.

-     Architect & Contractor: Landlord's generally like to have tenant finish work done by contractors with whom the landlord has a prior relationship and in some cases design professionals as well in order to maintain control of the process. However, it is critical for the tenant to obtain the right to use his contractor and design and construction professionals who are experienced and qualified in medical design and build-out as well as maintain some control in the management of the design and construction process.

-     Relocation Provision: It is common for office leases to contain provisions requiring the tenant to consent to a substitute premises should the landlord decide that it is in the landlord's best interest to move the tenant from one suite in the building to another. Because of the specialized build-out needs of the medical tenant, medical tenants should resist these provisions.

-     Liens: As a result of the cost of medical leasehold improvements, physician practices often finance leasehold improvement costs above the landlord allowance as well as medical equipment purchases. Lien rights provided to the Landlord should be subordinate to the Tenant's lenders for medical equipment purchases.

-     Restoration of Premises: Virtually all office space and retail leases contain provisions addressing the Landlord's and Tenant's rights and responsibilities regarding restoration obligations at the end of the lease. These provisions need to dovetail with the special situation of a medical tenant.

For the medical user real estate is a significant multi-year financial commitment, utilizing a knowledgeable real estate advisor and careful planning can insure selection of the right location and a well-structured transaction and lease agreement to fit the unique needs of the healthcare provider.

42. Future Topics

Dual Agency Laws

Starting in 2015 the commercial real estate industry will have another very hot topic written into law where brokers are now subject to Dual Agency Disclosure. Both Brokers and Sales agents will have to comply and acknowledge which side be it landlord, tenant, or both the agency or agencies that they represent. For Tenant Representation this is a major win and major selling point to companies that do not have a tenant representative on the tenant's side. Be on the lookout for new disclosure forms and with this information in hand contact your state bureau of real estate so you are in compliance and making it a point to know this cold.

Green Leases

This is one of the best websites to learn about the progressing Green Leases, <u>Green Lease Library</u>.

"What are Green Leases?

Green leases (also known as aligned leases, high performance leases, or energy efficient leases) align the financial and energy incentives of building owners and tenants so they can work together to save money, conserve resources, and ensure the efficient operation of buildings.

Why Are Green Leases Important?

Building leases lay out how energy costs are divided between tenants and owners. Often, these leases are not structured in a way that promotes energy savings. Under most gross leases, for example, tenants have no incentive to save energy in their leased premises because energy costs are based on tenant square footage. Under most net leases, building owners have no incentive to invest in efficiency for their building systems because the operating expenses are passed through to tenants, who would therefore receive all of the energy cost savings. Green leases promote energy efficiency by creating lease structures which equitably align the costs and benefits of efficiency investments between building owners and tenants.

About the Green Lease Library

This <u>website</u> is the result of a collaboration among several stakeholders in the green leasing community and is maintained by the Institute for Market Transformation (IMT). The website's purpose is to consolidate green leasing resources to provide a one-stop-shop for all audience types-- from building owners and tenants to lawyers and building raters. The green lease library is organized by resource type, and resources are tagged by relevance to audience and building types.

Made in the USA
Coppell, TX
03 November 2020